A GUIDE TO THE
RIMROCK DRIVE

COLORADO NATIONAL MONUMENT

BY ROSE HOUK

PUBLISHED BY COLORADO NATIONAL MONUMENT ASSOCIATION, FRUITA, COLORADO

*Copyright 1987 by Colorado National
    Monument Association*
*Editorial: Claudia Rector and
    Hank Schoch*
Design: McQuiston & Daughter, Inc.

Third Edition, 2000

ISBN #0-9679763-0-8

*Printed in the United States of America
Pyramid Printing, Grand Junction, Colorado*

*Photo Credits
Front cover, inside front and back
covers and photo this page by
Hank Schoch
Back cover by Michael Collier*

TO MY PARENTS

CONTENTS

4

SANDSTONE MONOLITHS IN MONUMENT CANYON, PHOTO BY HANK SCHOCH

INTRODUCTION

A s you begin to wind your way up the road into Colorado National Monument, you may be wondering what you are going to see. Is the monument some sort of concrete monolith, with elevators to carry you to the top? Or perhaps a memorial to an early pioneer who crossed the empty sagebrush flats searching for a homestead?

Instead, with each curve you begin to realize that you have come into a land set aside for its sheer magnificence. Colorado National Monument is a land of rock—balanced rocks, fallen rocks, red rocks, slick rocks, rocks that form sweeping arches and tapestries, and rocks that take the shapes of people and things you know.

To understand this land, you must switch gears to a time scale that goes far beyond human memory. The colorful sandstones and shales that form the cliffs and ledges had their origins in deserts, beaches, and rivers 200 million years ago. The rock that underlies it all is upwards of two billion years old—almost half the age of the Earth.

This land is also desert—a high, cold desert where winter temperatures can dip five degrees below zero and where summer temperatures can exceed 100 degrees. Moisture, or the lack thereof, is the limiting factor. The plants that have successfully adapted to the unpredictable conditions include shrubs, like sagebrush and saltbush. At higher elevations dwarf piñon and juniper trees take over, with mountain mahogany and serviceberry alongside. Woven through this mo-

5

saic are the threads of the streams, with their water-loving cottonwoods and willows. The streams are especially noticeable—and priceless—since they are so rare.

Water decides what lives here. Without water, plants are scarce, thus there is little organic material with which to build soils. All begins with bedrock. Technicolor lichens start the breakdown of rock. As soil sifts into cracks in a rock, the grasses, then larger shrubs, find a home in which to sink their roots.

Storms from both the north and the south meet here. Masses of clouds bump up against the high plateau, and in summer whopping downpours dispatch flashfloods down usually dry creek beds. In winter a soft frosting of snow outlines the red rock, and ice crystals trace the creeks.

Summers are hot, and winters are cold. Spring is the most fickle season in this desert: weeks of warm sunshine can be followed by blustery winds and snow.

But by spring you notice the purple flowers of vetch hugging the shoulders of the Rimrock Drive. A dash of lipstick-red Indian paintbrush peeks from beneath a gray-green rabbitbrush. A canyon wren hidden in an overhang treats you to its waterfall trill.

What you have found in Colorado National Monument is a place of infinite shape, sight, sound, and smell. A place to renew your spirit and clear your mind.

6

COLORADO PLATEAU

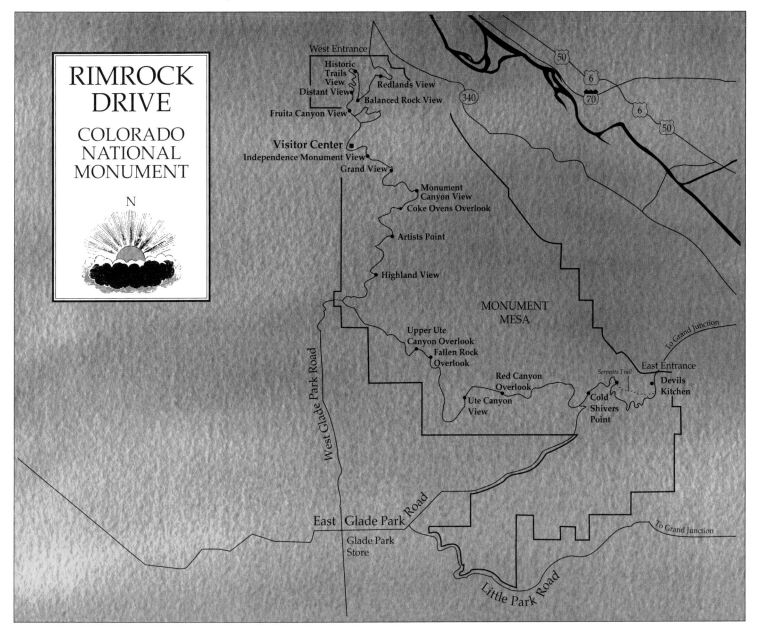

RIMROCK
DRIVE

COLORADO
NATIONAL
MONUMENT

N

West Entrance

Historic
Trails
View
Distant View
Redlands View
Balanced Rock View
Fruita Canyon View

Visitor Center
Independence Monument View
Grand View

Monument
Canyon View
Coke Ovens Overlook

Artists Point

Highland View

MONUMENT
MESA

Upper Ute
Canyon Overlook
Fallen Rock
Overlook

Red Canyon
Overlook
Ute Canyon
View

Serpents Trail
East Entrance
Cold
Shivers
Point
Devils
Kitchen

To Grand Junction

West Glade Park Road

East Glade Park Road

Glade Park
Store

To Grand Junction

Little Park Road

340

50

6

70

6

50

7

8

(Facing page) Workmen with Depression-era agencies such as the Civilian Conservation Corps, Works Progress Administration and others, as well as skilled local workers hewed Rimrock Drive out of the sheer sandstone walls in Colorado National Monument. Much of the job involved hard manual labor, chipping at the rock with picks and shovels, then trucking it away. The CCCers were fed and housed in camps at the Monument. Conditions were good for the most part, with a notable exception in the winter of 1936. The water line to the camps froze and the men went without baths for two months. It took the entire winter for the line to thaw.

(This page) Blasting was the first step in removing the rock before the men could come in with hand tools. In 1933 disaster struck when nine local workmen were killed in a tragic blasting accident just before Christmas. Photos courtesy of the National Park Service.

9

10

CLOSEUP, MONUMENT CANYON IN WINTER, NPS PHOTO BY HANK SCHOCH

RIMROCK DRIVE

This book is a guide to the Rimrock Drive, a 23-mile (37-km) paved road through Colorado National Monument. The guide assumes you will begin your visit at the West Entrance and travel east. If, instead, you came in through the East Entrance, the one nearer Grand Junction, then simply read the booklet from back to front.

More than a dozen signed viewpoints and overlooks along the road are included in this book, though you may wish to stop at others as well. Use caution when entering and exiting pullouts. Maximum speed along the road is 35 miles (56 km) per hour.

The Visitor Center, open all year, contains exhibits and publications that provide more information about the Monument. Also, check there for the schedule of interpretive programs given by park rangers.

Driving through the park is one way to gain an appreciation of it. Another is walking. Included at the end of this guide is a brief section that describes hiking trails in the Monument.

12

APPLE-PICKING IN THE GRAND VALLEY, PHOTO COURTESY OF COLORADO HISTORICAL SOCIETY

REDLANDS VIEW

John Otto, the most fervent supporter Colorado National Monument has ever known, proclaimed of the Grand Valley that "Our sunshine is the sunniest, our soil is the richest; our pumpkins are as big as railroad oil tanks and our peaches are as big as the moon."

Otto uttered this enthusiastic exclamation about his newly adopted home in the early part of this century. Some years before, William E. Pabor must have had the same feeling. He founded the small town of Fruita, nestled in the Grand Valley across the Colorado River below you.

Pabor, organizer of the Fruita Town and Land Company, planted 110 acres of bottomland in fruit trees in the spring of 1884. Despite the valley's long growing season and fertile soil, Pabor knew that nothing would grow here without water. He bought rights to it and set about seeing that canals were dug to bring it to Fruita's orchards and fields.

Within three months of his arrival, Pabor saw Fruita blossom from a single log cabin to include a school, railroad station, general store, hotel, blacksmith shop, and post office. Prosperous though the town may have seemed to people in those days, an item in the *Fruita Star* in 1889 puts some of its rapid progress in historical perspective. Emma Pabor advertised to buy a fresh milk cow, stating matter-of-factly that she wanted "no kicking beast or wild range animal." In payment for the cow and her calf Mrs. Pabor offered what was most plentiful—a fifty-foot residence lot in the new town.

Fruita apples took big prizes at shows in Denver at the turn of the century. By the 1920s, however, orchardists began to face a problem that early developers had not foreseen. Freezing temperatures and the worms of codling moths were wreaking havoc among their apple and pear crops. In the face of the destruction, the fruit trees were cut down and replaced by fields of alfalfa and barley.

The area on this side of the Colorado River, the Redlands, saw little development. Stockmen drove their cattle across the hills, and a few orchards were planted, but that was about all. Now subdivisions nuzzle the Monument boundaries, with a 20,534-acre playground for their backyard.

13

14

CATTLE DRIVE ON THE FRUITA DUGWAY, CIRCA 1920, PHOTO COURTESY OF NATIONAL PARK SERVICE

HISTORIC TRAILS VIEW

Look hard at the wall of the canyon across from you. A faint line midway down the sheer, orange cliff traces the course of a dugway, or trail, built before the turn of the century.

The townspeople of Fruita had quickly realized that the muddy Colorado River wasn't fit to drink and that they must seek their domestic water elsewhere. They looked far—to springs on Piñon Mesa, twenty-three miles away.

The dugway, now little more than a hint of its former self, was carved into the cliff. Wagons soon bumped over it, hauling up the materials for a pipeline that would carry the pure high-country water to the town.

Redwood, of which the original line was built, was ferried across the river before the bridge was built. Or materials were swung across in a cage that slid on a cable over the river. Metal later replaced most of the wooden pipeline, but remnants of the original can be glimpsed along the Rimrock Drive.

The first cattlemen judged the Grand Valley to be prime country for wintering their herds. After the water pipeline was finished, ranchers used the dugway to move their stock from Piñon Mesa and Glade Park to the grass-filled valley below. Their gangly drift fences, built as temporary corrals, can still be found in the Monument.

Glade Park rancher Don Roth drove his cattle up and down in spring and fall and remembers the dugway as a "tortuous" route. Other big outfits ran their cattle in the valley and across the state line into the deserts of eastern Utah. Families like the Youngs, Taylors, Turners, and Browns were some of them—names that no doubt sprouted up at the annual Cowpuncher's Ball in Fruita.

These were no rhinestone cowboys. As drover Charles Moore recalled, "The day extended from when you was able to see a cow in the morning until it got so dark you couldn't see her at night." Like cowboys everywhere, they ate the dust, endured the pestilential gnats and unpredictable weather, and raised a little Cain on paydays.

Those were the times of nasty encounters between sheepmen and cattlemen, some of which ended in death. Cattle rustlers were as popular as coyotes, and often earned the same fate. A deputy found one unlucky gang in Westwater Canyon, downstream from Fruita, and sent word "to send five cheap coffins."

The dugway, about a cow's-width wide, has seen few cattle drives in recent years. The old cowboys would probably scratch their heads in wonder that people now walk the dugway for sheer fun.

15

16

THE BOOK CLIFFS, PHOTO BY RICK NOLAN

DISTANT VIEW

To Colorado River explorer John Wesley Powell they looked like the edge of a bound book, so he named them the Book Cliffs. In the distance before you, the pleats of the Book Cliffs spill down to the floor of the Grand Valley.

The gray clay of the Book Cliffs is the Mancos Shale, accumulating in places to thicknesses of 1,500 feet above the valley. Topped with a layer of sandstone, the cliffs are protected from weathering. But once that cap is gone, the shale is worn down into gullied badlands—known locally as the adobe hills—that appear totally bereft of life.

This is true for most of the year, but in March, April, and May the hills spring to life with ephemeral plants—those that rush into bloom if blessed with sufficient winter moisture. Yellow beeplant, phacelia, and desert yarrow are among them.

The Book Cliffs are known in other circles for their rich coal seams. This hardened rock was once the muck of swamps on the edge of the shifting sea that laid down the Mancos Shale and Mesa Verde Sandstone. The swamp muck included decaying plants and animals that ultimately were transformed into the black bituminous fuel. In 1894, 150 tons of coal were shipped from the Book Cliff Mine, and Mesa County hoped to become the leading coal producer of the region. The coal boom was short-lived, however, and most mines in the Book Cliffs are inactive today. Whether that will remain true for long depends on events far removed from western Colorado. From the foot of Grand Mesa, the Book Cliffs extend like a great wall all the way to Price, Utah, 150 miles as the crow flies, but more than 250 miles if you were to follow their sinuous, S-shaped curve.

17

18

AERIAL VIEW OF THE FRUITA CANYON MONOCLINE, PHOTO BY MICHAEL COLLIER

FRUITA CANYON VIEW

Geologically speaking, Colorado National Monument is on the frontier. It lies on the northeastern edge of the Colorado Plateau, a mile-high province of horizontal, sedimentary rock cut by deep canyons. The Plateau's 130,000 square miles cover parts of Colorado, Utah, New Mexico, and Arizona. And *this* is where the Plateau begins.

Although the rock of the Plateau remains remarkably untouched by Earth's restiveness, sometimes it breaks, bends, and is shoved up in a seeming quest to exceed already dazzling heights.

When rocks bend, as they have done in Fruita Canyon, they can form what is called a monocline—a one-sided fold that has been launched but that hasn't come down. You can read about monoclines in geology textbooks, but one of the few places in the world where you can see them in abundance is on the Colorado Plateau. The best way to appreciate one is to feel it in your heart, lungs, and hamstrings. Once you've walked *up* a monocline, you will have no problem understanding what one is.

To complicate matters, the rock has not only bent, it has also broken. Such breaks, called faults, some very old and very deep, underlie the entire northern margin of Colorado National Monument.

The Colorado Plateau actually is made up of a series of several plateaus. This one is called the Uncompahgre, which to the Ute Indians means "place where water makes red rock."

In recent geologic time, perhaps eight million years ago or less, the Uncompahgre Plateau was uplifted. This wasn't the first time the Uncompahgre had staged an uprising. Much earlier, about 300 million years ago, it was a major mountain range.

It is a maxim of geology that high places erode. In keeping with this law, all the Paleozoic rocks were shed from Uncompahgria, the ancient Uncompahgre upland. Once leveled, the surface saw new rocks deposited. First was a shale called the Chinle Formation. If you place your hand on the line where the bright red slopes of the Chinle rest on the dark basement rock in Fruita Canyon, you are spanning more than a billion years. All the rock from that interval of time has been removed from the record here.

The so-called basement rock hails from the Precambrian era. Once sedimentary rock like the rock you are standing on, it was placed under extreme heat and pressure and was changed, or metamorphosed, into schist and gneiss. Its contorted crystalline face reveals its great age. Plugs of molten rock intruded it and slowly cooled into pink granite. The granite has been dated at 1.7 billion years, and the schists and gneisses are even older.

19

20

JOHN OTTO, FOUNDING FATHER OF COLORADO NATIONAL MONUMENT, PHOTO COURTESY OF NATIONAL PARK SERVICE

OTTO'S TRAIL

Those who knew John Otto often remarked about his eyes: piercing-blue and "vacant," one woman said. Most people in kindness considered him eccentric, but some believed that he might be half-crazy, living like he did in the canyons, with only his burros for company.

But no one ever accused him of failing to love his home. He adopted the canyons of Colorado National Monument as his residence, and he asked little of anyone else except the same undying allegiance to the place.

As soon as he arrived in the Grand Valley in 1906, John enthusiastically joined the campaign to have part of the splendid canyon country set aside as a park. To build his trails and roads he wrote letters to leaders in Washington, bombarded the Grand Junction newspaper with correspondence, and collected small sums of money from Mesa Countians. On May 24, 1911, President William Howard Taft declared the area a national monument.

An inordinate amount of debate ensued over its name. True to his desire that all Americans visit the new reserve, Otto proposed "Smith National Monument Park." His rationale was that such a designation would bring millions of Smiths flocking to see their namesake. Various other names were bandied about until the present one was finally chosen.

Otto interrupted his work long enough to marry Beatrice Farnham, an artist from New England who had also been captured by the beauty and wide open spaces of the West. She accepted John's engagement gift—a burro—and took her wedding vows at the base of Independence Monument.

Alas, the marriage was brief. After only a few months, Beatrice left John and returned to the East. They were soon divorced, but John never once disparaged his former wife. "She had no faults," he said, "only she couldn't stand the dizzy heights." Others speculated that Beatrice could not abide the burros that shared their tent-home.

While serving as the Monument's first custodian, John decided that the place needed more wildlife. With buffalo nickels donated by school children, he bought three bison and introduced them into the Monument. Fenced inside their new home, the buffalo went forth and multiplied and quickly ate themselves out of house and home. The Monument's grasses and sagebrush could not sustain the hungry herd, and all the animals finally were removed in 1983.

In 1927, a year after he had introduced the bison, John Otto resigned as custodian of the Monument. By the early 1930s he moved away, never to return to his sacred canyon country. He died in northern California at the age of seventy-three and is buried there.

21

22

INDEPENDENCE MONUMENT, PHOTO BY HANK SCHOCH

INDEPENDENCE MONUMENT

Independence Monument rests on shaky ground. Its base is the bright red rock of the Chinle Formation. You've seen the Chinle before in the park as the slopes beneath the sandstone cliffs. It is soft rock that erodes easily, not the kind you would think capable of supporting this 550-foot-high monolith.

Possibly someday, though probably not in our lifetimes or our children's, Independence Monument could topple to the ground. But we don't need to worry just yet. For Independence Monument has weathered a great deal and stood up over a very long time.

Consider how it was formed. From one perspective this monolith looks first like a slender spire. From another view it appears stockier, likened by one geologist to a bridge pier. This second angle tells the most accurate story. Independence Monument was carved over eons from a solid wall that separated Monument and Wedding canyons. It is an orphaned chunk of that wall that has not yet given in to the gnawing and battering of water and wind and ice.

Other monoliths near Independence, with such descriptive names as Praying Hands, Organ Pipe, and Kissing Couple, have formed in much the same way. They consist substantially of Wingate Sandstone, the cliff-forming rock in the Monument. The buff-colored Wingate is the product primarily of windblown sand dunes that blew in from the northwest about 200 million years ago. Beautiful swirls of crossbeds in the Wingate tell of its origin and the direction the wind was blowing.

That Independence Monument maintains its stature is due to a caprock—the Kayenta Formation—that is protecting it from destruction. Streams flowing across the Wingate dunes deposited mud, sand, and gravel. These sediments were then cemented with calcite and silica into the whitish to purplish Kayenta Formation. It is the silica that provides the tough glue that holds the Kayenta in place. Though present in the Monument in much thinner layers than the Wingate Sandstone, the Kayenta nevertheless is an important influence on the shape of the land. The beehive-shaped Coke Ovens give a good idea of what Independence Monument might look like without its Kayenta cap.

Chinle, Wingate, and Kayenta. The list is not complete without a fourth, the Entrada Sandstone. The Entrada also was the product of sand dunes. Bordering the Rimrock Drive through this part of the Monument, it is easily identified by its rounded contours and solution cavities. Entrada is the trade name for what is known generically all over the canyon country simply as slickrock.

23

24

COLORADO RIVER THROUGH THE GRAND VALLEY, PHOTO BY MICHAEL COLLIER

GRAND VIEW

A bit of history helps to explain the common denominator of so many names in this part of the country. Grand Junction, Grand Mesa, Grand Valley. . . . They are all due to the Grand River, you see.

What we now call the Colorado River here was once the Grand River. Early geologists like Henry Gannett, topographer in charge of a division of the far-flung Hayden Survey of the 1870s, wrote that "the Grand emerges into that great valley which is known here as the Grand River Valley."

The Colorado River existed then also, but it did not begin until the Grand and the Green met in Utah. Some people consider the Colorado's source to be in the Wind River Mountains in Wyoming, where the Green River begins. Others, especially in the state of Colorado, believe that it begins in Rocky Mountain National Park, the source of Gannett's Grand River.

The disagreement is a hydrologic one. The Green is longer, but the Grand was bigger in volume. The state of Colorado won in 1921 when it succeeded in having the Grand River renamed the Colorado. This became more than a scientific question a year later when a compact was signed that divided the water in the Colorado River among the seven states in its basin.

The town of Grand Junction was laid out in 1881 at the confluence of the Gunnison and what was then the Grand River. Still Ute Indian Reservation, however, the land could not be officially settled for another year. After the Utes were removed, a rush was on for choice ranch and farm lands. Irrigation canals were dug immediately. The Denver and Rio Grande Railroad came the same year, providing the necessary transportation for crops to reach markets.

Businesses thrived in the new town, but all (including the twenty-two saloons) closed every Sunday afternoon at two o'clock, long enough for "Miss Nannie," the school teacher, to read the scriptures. Once that was done, business proceeded as usual.

The underpinning of Grand Junction's economy has always been agriculture. Lately farmers and orchardists have been experiencing problems with salt accumulation in the soil. Even as early as 1874, geologist Gannett had reported that the valley soil was "a stiff, adhesive, bottomless clay, containing considerable alkali." Irrigation has worsened the problem, since poorly drained soils and evaporation tend to concentrate the salts. Ditches are being lined and fields are being leveled and drained to help solve the problem.

To the east the "highest flat-topped mountain in the world," Grand Mesa, presides over the valley. Its 11,000-foot heights are covered with trout-filled lakes and forests of spruce, fir, and aspen. A resistant basalt layer accounts for its tabletop flatness.

25

26

MONUMENT CANYON SUNRISE, PHOTO BY HANK SCHOCH

MONUMENT CANYON AND COKE OVENS

Monument Canyon may well lay claim to being the heart of Colorado National Monument. A large and accessible canyon, it beckons for a closer look.

"But how do you get down there?" you might well ask. We have John Otto to thank. He built a trail in true Otto style—it doesn't go anywhere very quickly, and offers a fine day's ramble below the rim.

But John knew where he was going with the Monument Canyon Trail. As you round a bend, the trail leads right up to the hulking base of Independence Monument. From this perspective, you more fully appreciate the monolith's magnitude. For reasons known only to John Otto, he and his wife Beatrice inscribed the words "John Hancock" and the last lines of the Declaration of Independence on a large slab near its base. For the Fourth of July celebration in 1910, with typical patriotic fervor, John scaled Independence Monument and planted the Stars and Stripes at the top.

Though the flag no longer flies, Monument Canyon still contains some wonderful surprises, even in midwinter. A bladderpod shyly opens its bright yellow flowers in eager anticipation of spring. Winterfat, rabbitbrush, and fendlerbush lend their russets, grays, and browns to the winter landscape. Milky water flows down the creek, and delicate, heart-shaped deer tracks are impressed in the wet sand. A side-blotched lizard reclines on a rock, soaking up some high-noon sun. Phosphorescent green moss, normally dark and desiccated, sponges up snowmelt. The possibility of a mountain lion's presence adds a measure of hopeful suspense.

The Monument Canyon Trail starts from the Rimrock Drive. If you haven't time for a long stroll, you can bear right on the trail for a short walk to the Coke Ovens overlook. In autumn, below the rim, the late afternoon sun makes the salmon-colored walls appear to glow from within. The remaining few leaves of the serviceberry hang from branches like gold coins. A spring flows silently from a crevice, creating a climate where water-loving ferns and columbines can exist.

Each place here has special qualities, and each differs depending on the season. The rim offers outstanding panoramas of the big features. Below the rim are the smaller, more intimate nooks and crannies, waiting to be discovered.

27

28

THE FOSSIL-RICH MORRISON FORMATION, PHOTO BY HANK SCHOCH

ARTIST'S POINT

he slender colorful beds of the Wanakah Formation behind you have invited their comparison to an artist's paint palette. While aesthetic appreciation is certainly important, paleontologists look at these colors and think of bones – dinosaur bones. They know that just on top of the Wanakah rests the thicker Morrison Formation.

On the Colorado Plateau the Morrison is synonymous with dinosaurs. It was laid down during the age of the thundering lizards, some 135 million years ago. At that time Colorado National Monument was like a tropical forest, lush with cycads, ferns, and sequoia trees growing beside streams and lakes and swamps.

Elmer S. Riggs was one scientist who came here, on the advice of a local dentist, who told him he would find dinosaur bones in the Morrison. During the summer of 1900 Riggs quarried in the clay and sandstone hills in the shadow of Colorado National Monument. He found a partial skeleton of *Brachiosaurus*, then believed to be the largest animal that ever sauntered on Earth. *Brachiosaurus* was a large beast. The thigh bone alone was taller than a man. The monstrous bones that Riggs unearthed, encased in plaster cocoons, were hauled out in wagons and shipped by rail to the Field Museum in Chicago to be reconstructed.

Riggs returned the following year and dug along the Colorado River near Fruita. This time he found the vertebrae, ribs, pelvis, and leg bones of *Brontosaurus*, now known as *Apatosaurus*. Since Riggs's initial excavations, remains of at least five other kinds of dinosaurs, both large and small, have been found by others working in the area.

Recently a nearby area has yielded not only fossils of large dinosaurs but also bones of tiny early mammals. The occurrence of both these animals together at one site is significant, according to Dr. George Callison, head of the excavation project. Fieldwork has changed little since the days when Elmer Riggs was here. On hands and knees with their noses on the outcrops, Callison and his crew have searched for the treasures locked in the Morrison.

29

PIÑON PINE, PHOTO BY HANK SCHOCH

HIGHLAND VIEW

For the last few miles you have been climbing. You have reached 6,000 feet above sea level, and not too much farther on a sign marks the highest elevation on the Rimrock Drive—6,640 feet.

In the absence of a sign, there is another, fairly reliable way to judge elevation in the Monument. When the piñon trees begin to take over, you can be sure that you are close to 6,000 feet. These short-needled pines, characteristic of highlands in the Southwest, extend from this elevation up to about 8,500 feet. The Utah junipers, their forest associates, dominate at lower elevations.

Early Southwest explorers came to appreciate the piñon because it saved their lives. In 1776 three Ute women gave the Spanish padres Domínguez and Escalante piñon nuts and chokecherries to eat as they were passing through this part of Colorado.

By the time the holy men had reached the Grand Canyon in October, they were so weak with hunger that they bought more than a bushel of the rich seeds from Indians. So impressed were they with the piñon nut that on the final map of their journey they showed the Southwest as a "Land of mesas covered with trees that give a fine pine nut. . ."

In good years the sticky, stubby cones burst with nuts. Since the seeds lack wings, they depend on other means for dispersal. It is primarily to piñon jays that the tree owes its regeneration.

These raucous, social birds are an integral part of the piñon forest. Beginning in late August when the cones are still closed, they start gathering them, removing the seeds, and caching them near their nesting areas. Piñon researcher Ronald Lanner has discovered that the jays can tell by sound, sight, and weight that tan seeds are empty but dark brown ones are full.

Though *Pinus edulis* is well adapted to live in arid places, its seeds cannot germinate in full sun. Conveniently, piñon jays bury the seeds in moist soil. If the jay doesn't return or if rodents or people don't find the cache first, the seeds can sprout and become viable trees.

In Professor Lanner's words, "Tree feeds bird and bird plants tree." It is a beautiful example of symbiosis in nature: two organisms that have evolved together for the good of both.

The ecology of the piñon forest goes far beyond this, however. The trees provide cover for mule deer, winter food for porcupines, and breeding areas for the gray flycatcher and plain titmouse. An insect, the piñon spindle gall midge, builds its home on piñon branches and midge larvae munch the fresh green tissue. Piñon mice and rock squirrels eat the seeds, and the sawfly its needles. A parasitic dwarf mistletoe has even found a niche on piñons, causing a blister rust disease on the trees.

31

FALLEN ROCK, SLUMPED OFF UTE CANYON WALL, PHOTO BY MICHAEL COLLIER

FALLEN ROCK VIEW

No one knows when Fallen Rock slumped to the floor of Ute Canyon. Possibly people were here to see it, even if it happened thousands of years ago, but they left no written record.

People have lived in these canyons for a very long time. The earliest ones were solely hunters and gatherers. But by A.D. 400 in parts of the Southwest they began to settle down and supplement nature's wild crops with domestic ones of their own.

Remains found in this part of the Colorado Plateau are from people called the Fremont, named for the Fremont River in their homeland in Utah. The Monument is as far east as their traces have been found, and evidence of their presence here is slight.

Though they never gave up hunting and gathering entirely, the Fremont did farm this land. To catch water running off slopes during rainstorms, they built rock checkdams in drainages. Alcoves in the cliffs provided good storage places for corn. Due to the dry climate, remarkably well-preserved corn has been found after eight centuries.

The Fremont people have presented a persistent problem to archaeologists. They exhibit some traits of their own as well as ones of other major cultural groups, leading to something of an identity crisis for them. Like their Anasazi neighbors to the south, the Fremont had the bow and arrow, pottery, and basketry. They also showed some traits, such as hide shields, that reflect influence from Plains people.

Though they sometimes settled in small villages, their architecture was crude in comparison to that of the famous cliff-dwellers of Mesa Verde. Their pottery was a plain gray that never achieved the artistry of the Anasazi's.

But archaeologists have also identified artifacts unique to the Fremont. They fashioned moccasins of animal hide that had dewclaws attached. Bighorn sheep, no doubt highly valued animals, were frequently depicted in their rock art, the most outstanding evidence the Fremont left behind. Some of the drawings are pecked into the dark coating on the rock; others are painted. The distinctive element of Fremont rock art is a broad-shouldered humanlike figure. Often they have eyes, and are adorned with necklaces, earrings, or sashes. Many hold shields or have horns. Were these shamans, or beings with supernatural powers?

The demise or disappearance of the Fremont is as mysterious as their origins. By A.D. 1250 or 1300 they were gone from Colorado and Utah. Drought or enemies may have been their downfall, though this remains a matter of speculation, not only for the Fremont but also for several other groups who abandoned the region at about the same time.

33

34

DESERT VARNISH, UTE CANYON, PHOTO BY HANK SCHOCH

UTE CANYON OVERLOOK

We have left our ancestors in the rocks. . . . The ancestors are watching over those mountains for us. Someday they will tell us when to go back.
—War Cry on a Prayer Feather, *Nancy Wood*

The Ute Indians have been in Colorado for a long, long time. It is only fitting that this canyon, which they may have passed through, should carry their name.

The domain of the Utes once encompassed half of Utah and two-thirds of Colorado. Now three small tribes remain on reservations in Utah and southern Colorado.

The Utes found nearly everything they needed here. Families spent summers in the mountains, and in the fall they moved down to the valleys and joined in winter encampments which were great social affairs. The Book Cliffs, the Grand Valley, and the canyons in and around Colorado National Monument were all their old stomping grounds.

Fathers Domínguez and Escalante skirted the edge of Grand Mesa in 1776. They were looking for Indians who grew corn, but instead found the Utes in their traditional hunting grounds. The Utes were not especially interested in farming when their land was rich with game.

If they needed shelter, they built circular brush-and-pole structures called wickiups. Families that could afford ten elk or buffalo hides built tipis, like their Plains neighbors. People in camp kept busy tanning buckskin and buffalo hides for moccasins and blankets. Venison hung on drying racks, and baskets were set out, covered with pine pitch for waterproofing.

After the Spaniards introduced the horse to them, the nomadic Utes became even more mobile. A man's wealth was judged by the number of horses he owned. They could ride to the Plains and hunt bison, and trade the valuable buffalo robes at posts like Antoine Robidoux's near present-day Delta, Colorado.

As they traveled through the plains, mountains, and plateaus, the Utes, like the Fremont before them, left their mark in the form of artwork on rocks. Perhaps to give themselves luck in the hunt, they painted scenes of Indians on horseback shooting bison.

The names of Ute ancestors are imprinted on this country—Ouray, the great chief of the Utes; Atchee, chief of a local band of Utes; and Uncompahgre.

Archaeologists cannot say with certainty exactly where they came from or how long the Utes have lived in Colorado. The Utes themselves claim to be the oldest continuous residents of the state, and that when their ancestors tell them, they will return.

35

AERIAL VIEW OF RED CANYON, PHOTO BY MICHAEL COLLIER

RED CANYON

A black bear, groggy with winter sleep, ambles down from the high country of Glade Park to the rim of Red Canyon. The fat stored in her body is nearly gone, and she is exhausted by the demands of her voracious cubs. But she must continue to feed them a while longer.

Black bears have been seen at Red Canyon and other places in the Monument, though sightings are rare. They don't stay here, for they are truly animals of the mountains.

Visitors to the desert often wonder if any animals live here. Large mammals, which cause the greatest excitement, are often difficult to find. They are here, though most stay in hiding during the daytime. But a ride around the Rimrock Drive at dusk or early morning should result in a few sightings.

Gray foxes come up from the canyons to the rim at night in search of a supper of rodent, rabbit, or lizard. Mule deer, whose long ears have earned them their name, are commonly seen in early evening in the meadows and woodlands, nibbling grasses and shrubs. At the slightest sound of human presence, they stop eating and stare alertly. When certain that you mean no harm, they bend their heads to the ground and continue to graze. Mountain lions, bobcats, and coyotes are also present.

Smaller animals, like the rodents and bats, are the real success stories here. In his studies in the park, biologist Pat Miller reported that the diminutive deer mouse was the most abundant mammal, found in nearly all habitats and at all elevations. Along with pocket mice, canyon mice, harvest mice, packrats, chipmunks, and squirrels, they are the backbone of the environment. Without them, the owls and hawks and snakes and coyotes would be long gone.

Because there is potential for conflict over the desert's limited food resources, mice divide the habitat to reduce competition. While one species eats the seeds under a bush, another opts for those scattered about in the open, and yet another will burrow underground for food.

Bats—the only mammals that can fly—also provide interesting examples of this partitioning. One way that they apparently share the wealth is to stagger their foraging trips. Like the mice, they specialize in where and what they eat. Shadows across their roosts trigger the nighttime foraging flights of western pipistrelles, the most common bat in the Monument. In late evening these slow erratic flyers make their way downcanyon toward the Colorado River for insects. Pipistrelles stop feeding about two hours after sundown and come out again at dawn.

A bear? Perhaps. But there is much more here to be seen, if we adjust our habits to those of the animals.

37

38

GOLDEN EAGLE, MONARCH OF THE SKY, PHOTO BY JOHN RUNNING

COLD SHIVERS POINT

No one can tell me that ravens don't play. I have watched them, as they somersault over the canyons. Either alone or with a friend, they engage in aerobatics that are nearly unexcelled in the bird world. And ravens are smart. They have watched me as I have them, and by their squawking and croaking they let me know I have been seen. I believe those who say they are the most intelligent of all birds.

The common raven is found nearly everywhere in both cold and hot climates. But it is the quintessential desert bird—tough, crafty, and not given to luxuriousness. With other members of their family—the jays and magpies—they are seen nearly everywhere here.

The ravens' black coloring is believed to be an advantage, making them visible and possibly alerting other ravens that their table has just been set with the carcass of a jackrabbit.

Biologist Bernd Heinrich has observed ravens calling to one another when food is located. Why would a raven want to share with its brethren? Heinrich says that "cooperation is common in the animal world, and it is often the key to survival in hostile environments." This sharing behavior, in a desert environment, ultimately assures the survival of all, rather than one.

The brazen ravens also chase golden eagles, but the eagles seem somehow superior and more dignified than their playful tormentors. In comparison, an eagle's 6½ to 7½-foot wingspan exceeds that of a large raven's by a third. They float on the thermals, with alternating wingbeats that are obviously more powerful even than the raven's.

The eagles will soar for hours over the sandstone monoliths and mesas, searching for prey. When food has been sighted, these skilled hunters dive at speeds estimated at 150 miles an hour. Their usual fare includes rabbits and ground squirrels, but like ravens they are also carrion-eaters. They have been known to capture ravens on the wing.

Less obvious but no less talented a flier is the common nighthawk. The canyon abysses serve as excellent stages for its performances. Although normally silent, nighthawk sounds mark the arrival of summer in the desert. Just returned from the south, they begin the mating season in earnest. To announce his presence to his chosen mate, the male sounds a nasal call and swoops down in ostentatious courting flights. As he bottoms out of a dive, the feathers of the pointed wings vibrate. The loud boom that results has earned the nighthawk the name "bullbat."

Nighthawks do not build nests, but simply lay their eggs on exposed ground. The males roost nearby while the females tend the eggs. In the evenings they leave their eggs to fly with the males for feasts of insects.

40

MODERN RIMROCK DRIVE AND HISTORIC SERPENTS TRAIL, PHOTO BY MICHAEL COLLIER

SERPENTS TRAIL

Most of us had never rode a train or been out of Texas," wrote Roy Hair, of Gilmer, Texas.

He was one of hundreds of young men sent from Texas, Oklahoma, and other states in the 1930's to help build the Rimrock Drive. They were enrollees in President Franklin D. Roosevelt's Depression-era Civilian Conservation Corps. Members of the CCC, as it was known, were fed, clothed, and housed in camps in the Monument. They joined members of other Depression-era agencies and skilled workers, many from the local area, to build the spectacular road.

With picks and shovels, dynamite and dumptrucks the workers built the road — out of sheer sandstone cliffs in many cases. Some men did nothing but swing sledgehammers all day, other skilled workers drilled "coyote holes" — short T-shaped blastholes — for the tunnels, while some drove the trucks and spread the rock fill.

As Roy Hair put it, "Everything was solid rock . . . . The work was hard and dangerous." The danger became reality in a sobering experience in December 1933. Nine road workers, most of them heads of families from nearby Glade Park and Fruita, were killed in a blasting accident at a tunnel just days before Christmas.

The CCCers were paid a wage of thirty-five to forty dollars a month, most of which was sent home to their families. The corps also helped to build several structures in the Monument, including the stone house at Saddlehorn Campground.

Work on Rimrock Drive proceeded from a point on top down both the east and west sides. By 1939, nineteen of twenty-three miles were complete, though not paved. The Park Service asked for more help, again through a federal relief project, to finish the work.

John Otto, the Monument's premier road and trailbuilder, was to have no part in construction of the Rimrock Drive. He left the Monument shortly after the government sent out its own surveyor.

John's road was the Serpents Trail, the predecessor of Rimrock Drive. He had laid out its path, and from about 1913 until 1921 helped build it. For Glade Park residents, the Serpents Trail was the main route from their ranches and farms to Grand Junction.

The twisting road was originally sixteen feet wide, "just enough for passing," according to John. Those who regularly negotiated the fifty-two hairpin curves on the Serpents Trail rarely had an uneventful trip. A spring along the route furnished water for overheated engines, and Charles and Catherine Moore said if they had to get out and push "we thought nothing about it."

The Serpents Trail remained open to vehicles until 1951. By that time the section of Rimrock Drive from Cold Shivers Point, down along No Thoroughfare Canyon, and out to the Monument's East Entrance was paved.

The Serpents Trail is now for foot travelers only.

41

GRACEFUL SWEEPS OF ENTRADA SANDSTONE, PHOTO BY HANK SCHOCH

HIKING TRAILS

Many miles of trails are available for hiking in Colorado National Monument, or you may wish to explore cross-country. None of the trails are accessible to the handicapped. Brief trail descriptions follow. For additional hiking information, consult staff at the Visitor Center. Topographic maps may also be purchased there. Please respect private property.

Always take plenty of water with you, since water sources may be contaminated and are not reliable. This is a desert, and in summer, water should account for most of the weight you carry. Overnight stays require a permit, available free at the visitor center. Horses are permitted in certain areas within the monument, check with staff at the Visitor Center. Hikers should yield the right-of-way to horses.

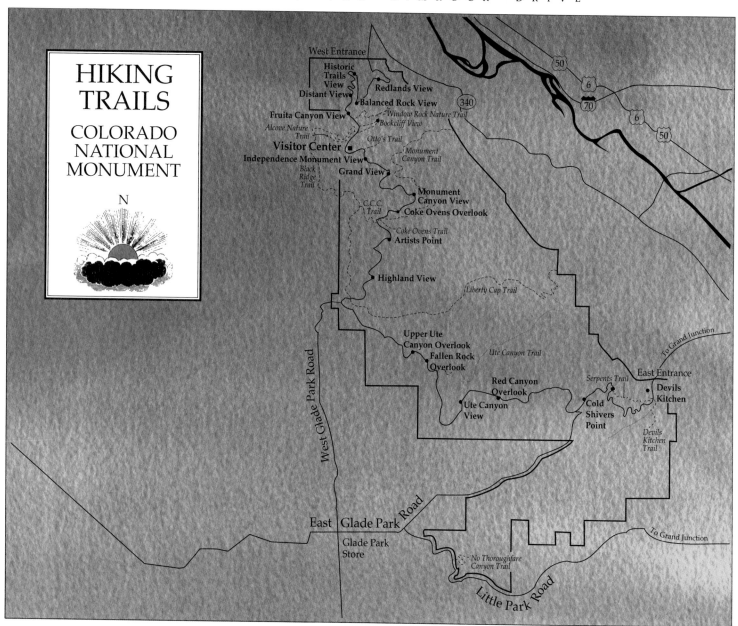

HIKING TRAILS

COLORADO NATIONAL MONUMENT

N

West Entrance
Historic Trails View
Distant View
Redlands View
Balanced Rock View
Fruita Canyon View
Window Rock Nature Trail
Bookcliff View
Alcove Nature Trail
Otto's Trail
Visitor Center
Monument Canyon Trail
Independence Monument View
Black Ridge Trail
Grand View
C.C.C. Trail
Monument Canyon View
Coke Ovens Overlook
Coke Ovens Trail
Artists Point
Highland View
Liberty Cap Trail
Upper Ute Canyon Overlook
Ute Canyon Trail
Fallen Rock Overlook
Red Canyon Overlook
Serpents Trail
East Entrance
Devils Kitchen
Ute Canyon View
Cold Shivers Point
Devils Kitchen Trail
West Glade Park Road
To Grand Junction
East   Glade Park   Road
Glade Park Store
No Thoroughfare Canyon Trail
To Grand Junction
Little Park Road

340
50
6
70
6
50

44

Carry out all your trash.

The following regulations apply to all backcountry users:

—No fires either on or below the rim. Use backpacker stoves.

—No firearms

—No pets

—No trail bikes or bicycles

The desert is fragile. Please travel lightly on it. Thank you.

WINDOW ROCK TRAIL

Roundtrip distance: 0.6 mi. (1 km)
Terrain: Gentle grade, improved surface
Features: Rimside views of Monument and Wedding Canyons, Grand Valley; piñon-juniper woodland
Trailhead: Saddlehorn Campground, Loop A, near Bookcliff Shelter

CANYON RIM TRAIL

Roundtrip distance: 1.0 mi. (1.6 km)
Terrain: Level, improved surface
Features: Follows the rim of Wedding Canyon
Trailhead: Visitor Center or Bookcliff Shelter

OTTO'S TRAIL

Roundtrip distance: 0.8 mi. (1.3 km)
Terrain: Gentle slope, improved surface
Features: Down backbone of rocky spur to promontory; overlooks Organ Pipe monolith, canyons, and Grand Valley
Trailhead: Otto's Trail Viewpoint, Rimrock Drive

MONUMENT CANYON TRAIL

Roundtrip distance: 12.2 mi. (19.6 km)
Terrain: Steep switchbacks 600 feet down into Monument Canyon from the rim. Moderate once in the canyon proper. Hike from mouth of canyon has moderate ascent.
Features: Good introduction to the heart of Colorado National Monument and to desert canyon hiking. Spectacular sandstone walls, monoliths
Trailhead: Upper, Monument Canyon Trail, Rimrock Drive; Lower, marked trailhead off Colorado 340 in Redlands.

COKE OVENS TRAIL

Roundtrip distance: 0.8 mi. (1.3 km)
Terrain: Switchbacks down short descent, then level along top of Kayenta Formation
Features: Closeup view of eroded sandstone formations called Coke Ovens
Trailhead: Monument Canyon Trail, Rimrock Drive

BLACK RIDGE TRAIL

Roundtrip distance: 11.2 mi. (18 km)
Terrain: Old road that climbs gradually to open, grassy ridge; requires crossing two fences; overlooks Devil's Canyon; clay surface difficult when wet

46

NATURAL ARCHES, UTE CANYON, PHOTO BY RICK NOLAN

Features: High elevation offers views of canyons, valleys, Grand Mesa, and on a clear day the San Juan Mountains ninety miles away; intermediate cross-country skiing

Trailhead: Liberty Cap/Black Ridge Trail; Rimrock Drive; also from Visitor Center

LIBERTY CAP TRAIL

Roundtrip distance: 14.0 mi. (22.5 km)

Terrain: Former motor nature trail to vantage point on rim; gently sloping across top of mesa; steep descent to valley

Features: Piñon-juniper, meadows, views of relatively remote sections of Monument; Liberty Cap formation on lower trail; beginning cross-country skiing trail

Trailhead: Upper, Liberty Cap Trail, Rimrock Drive; Lower, Wildwood Drive off South Broadway

UTE CANYON TRAIL

Roundtrip distance: 14.0 mi. (22.5 km)

Terrain: Steep descent on constructed trail from canyon rim, remainder follows Ute Canyon drainage

Features: Isolated, wild scenery; arch on south canyon wall; intermittent stream; seasonal pools

Trailhead: Upper, Ute Canyon Trail, Rimrock Drive; Lower, Wildwood Drive off South Broadway

SERPENTS TRAIL

Roundtrip distance: 4.0 mi. (6.4 km)

Terrain: Former roadway; steep, switch-backs

Features: Historic road called "crookedest in the world," built from 1921-1925; sandstone formations; view of No Thoroughfare Canyon

Trailhead: Lower, Devils Kitchen/Serpents Trail pullouts near East Entrance; Upper, Pullout above East Tunnel, Rimrock Drive

DEVILS KITCHEN TRAIL

Roundtrip distance: 1.4 (2.3 km)

Terrain: Gentle to moderate

Features: Exotic sandstone formations

Trailhead: Devils Kitchen pullout, Rimrock Drive; follow trail across No Thoroughfare Canyon

NO THOROUGHFARE CANYON TRAIL

Roundtrip distance: 17.0 (27.4 km)

Terrain: Canyon drainage; from mouth of canyon up to first waterfall, approximately two miles one way, easy; some scrambling to pass waterfalls, rough

Features: Through Precambrian schists and granites; seasonal waterfalls; stream-side vegetation

Trailhead: Lower, Devils Kitchen Trail, Rimrock Drive; Upper, Off Little Park Road in Glade Park, unmarked

ACKNOWLEDGMENTS

I would like to offer thanks to the staff of Colorado National Monument and the Colorado National Monument Association for allowing me the chance to write this guide. Claudia Rector, the Association's business manager, was a constant source of inspiration and enthusiasm. Board members Jim Johnson and Joe Hall made valuable comments to the manuscript.

I am also grateful to Hank Schoch, Chief of Interpretation, and to Beth Kaeding for sharing their knowledge and affection for "the Monument." I appreciate also Sally Cole's generous loan of materials on archaeology. Judy Prosser of the Museum of Western Colorado was especially helpful in locating historical photos.

Don and Debra McQuiston added their artistry in the book's design.

And to Michael, I owe more than I can ever say.

SUGGESTED READINGS

Armstrong, David M. *Mammals of the Canyon Country*. Canyonlands Natural History Association, Moab. 1982.

Baars, Donald L. *The Colorado Plateau: A Geologic History*. University of New Mexico Press, Albuquerque. 1983.

Cassells, E. Steve. *Archaeology of Colorado*. Johnson Books, Boulder. 1983.

Chronic, Halka. *Roadside Geology of Colorado*. Mountain Press, Missoula. 1979.

Kania, Alan J. *John Otto of Colorado National Monument*. Roberts Rinehart, Inc., Boulder. 1984.

Lanner, Ronald M. *The Piñon Pine: A Natural and Cultural History*. University of Nevada Press, Reno. 1981.

Lohman, S.W. *The Geologic Story of Colorado National Monument*. Geological Survey Bulletin 1508. U.S. Geological Survey, Washington, D.C. 1981.

Marsh, Charles S. *People of the Shining Mountains: The Utes of Colorado*. Pruett Publishing Co., Boulder. 1981.

Mehls, Steven F. *The Valley of Opportunity*. U.S. Bureau of Land Management. 1982.

Miller, Pat. *Colorado National Monument*. The Colorado–Black Canyon of the Gunnison Nature Association. 1969.

Ryser, Fred A., Jr. *Birds of the Great Basin*. University of Nevada Press, Reno. 1985.

Terres, John K. *The Audubon Society Encyclopedia of North American Birds*. Knopf, New York. 1980.

Vandenbusche, Duane and Duane A. Smith. *A Land Alone: Colorado's Western Slope*. Pruett Publishing Co., Boulder. 1981.

Wood, Nancy. *When Buffalo Free the Mountains*. Doubleday, New York. 1980.

Wormington, Marie. *A Reappraisal of the Fremont*. Denver Museum of Natural History. Proceedings No. 1., May 1, 1955.

Young, Robert G. and Joann W. Young. *Colorado West*. Robert G. Young. 1984.